Almost

As I remember it

TERRY GILL

authorHOUSE®

AuthorHouse™ UK
1663 Liberty Drive
Bloomington, IN 47403 USA
www.authorhouse.co.uk
Phone: UK TFN: 0800 0148641 (Toll Free inside the UK)
        UK Local: 02036 956322 (+44 20 3695 6322 from outside the UK)

Published by AuthorHouse 02/08/2021

ISBN: 978-1-6655-8489-0 (sc)
ISBN: 978-1-6655-8488-3 (hc)
ISBN: 978-1-6655-8490-6 (e)

Preface

This is the story, albeit a true one, of a group, a band, a pop group—call it what you will—that was started in the early sixties. We, like thousands of other groups that were formed at that time, wanted to be rich and famous and have everything that went with being a well-known pop star. It was the dream of 90 per cent of young men of the era.

I was helped in this endeavour by the other members of the group and people who were connected to the group, many of them from its inception to its demise. Unfortunately, age being what it is, our collective memories have been eroded by the passage of time; hence, the subtitle of this story—poetic licence.

Some names and places have been changed to protect privacy.

About 75 per cent of the bands that were formed around that time disbanded within a few months when they realised that you had to be able to play something or sing to be in a band. Another 20 per cent carried on and rehearsed and rehearsed, did a couple of gigs at the local pub, and then realised that it wasn't happening, or they were too busy at work, or their girlfriends didn't like it, so they knocked it on the head.

Unlike those bands, this band carried on and went for it and made it … well, almost.

Chapter 1

The Beginning

I suppose it was about 1964. I had a friend at school, Michael, whose nickname was Sam; we always call him Sam, never Michael. It was all to do with an old music hall star named Stanley Holloway, who used to sing, 'Sam, Sam, pick oop thy musket'. I can't really remember why—maybe it had been on TV or Sam kept singing it or something—but it was better than his original nickname, which was Wimpy after the character in Popeye. Anyway, Sam asked if I fancied starting a group. You must remember that, in 1964, every male between the ages of ten and fifteen wanted to be, or was, in a group of some sort. Well, having nothing better to do, and although I couldn't play any kind of instrument, I said yes.

We gathered a motley group of people who all thought the same. There was Dave Griffiths, a neighbour of Sam's. Sam and I had been to junior school with him, but he had gone on to grammar school, clever git that he was, whereas Sam and I went to the secondary school. Dave was always known as Griff from his last name, obviously a shortened version of Griffiths. Another member was Neil Bedford, who was in the same class as Sam and me. He was known as Nelly, and he was a strange boy who had lost an eye in a camping accident—it's a wonder we didn't nickname him Popeye, but that would have been cruel, wouldn't it? That made four members,

1

which seemed to be the norm for groups back then. Oh, the fourth member was me, Terry Gill. I don't think I had a nickname, unless it was Tosser.

We didn't have any instruments, apart from an old bass drum that Griff's father had played in the Boy Scouts band years before, so we painted guitars onto cardboard, cut them out to shape, and mimed to records in Griff's garage. It was good enough at the time. I thought I was really good at that—in fact, I played that cardboard guitar better than I can a real one! Nelly said he had a friend who could actually play guitar and wanted to join the group, so he came along. His name was Stan South. He lived in Nechells, which was a good bus ride away, so he must have been keen. The rest of us lived within a mile or so of each other on the Beeches Estate.

Well, Stan was a godsend. He could play two or three chords, which made him almost godlike. He was also a very nice guy—still is, although I don't see him that much nowadays—and at the time, that was more important than what he could do. He taught Sam the chords, so we now had two guitarists and one old guitar that Stan had brought along.

We also had a bass drum but no pedal and various plastic washing-up bowls that made up our drum kit. I was voted in as the drummer but had to supply my own drumsticks.

Griff at that time was going to play guitar, so Nelly acquired from somewhere an old beat-up Spanish guitar, and Sam got himself a guitar. I think the pair of them must have cost £5.

Nelly couldn't get his head around playing a guitar (neither could the rest of us, but someone had to do it), so he decided that he didn't want to play anything but would be our manager and photographer. We would walk around town doing silly poses while Nelly took pictures. Griff and I were both having problems with our chosen instruments—mainly that we couldn't play them—so we decided to *swap, Griff on drums and me on guitar. This didn't make a lot of difference, because we couldn't play those instruments either!*

Because the Spanish guitar that Nelly had gotten from the junk shop was so beat up, we thought that could be the bass guitar and that I could play bass. So we took off the normal strings and put on four bass strings. Looking back now, I wonder how the neck on that poor guitar never folded in half under the pressure of bass strings. But it didn't, so off we went.

We now had four band members, a manager, and instruments. Now all we had to do was learn how to play. I think we started rehearsing in Griff's garage but found it too cold so then went to Sam's front room. His mom and dad were the nicest people you would ever want to meet and supplied us with tea and sympathy. How they ever put up with it I'll never know—I think the fact that his dad was as deaf as a post probably helped.

We wanted to be different from the other fifty groups in the area, so we thought we'd write our own songs, which we did. Stan and Sam would go up to Sam's bedroom and come down five minutes later with two or three songs they had written. The only one I remember was entitled 'There Are Flowers at the Bottom of My Garden Stomp'. Sad bastard that I am, I can still remember how it goes. But unfortunately, I can't sing it here—shame.

Talking of singing, that was another of our problems. Not one of us could sing, not a note, so we had to find a singer. We found our singer in the form of Chris York, also known as Pongo. He got his nickname from a kids' TV programme about pirates and not because he smelt. He was another classmate of Sam and mine and a bit of a nutter. We thought he could come in handy when fronting a band, and also, he had a mouth organ, or gob iron as they were called. The fact that he couldn't play it was neither here nor there, so we had our singer. And we were to find out very soon that he couldn't sing either.

After rehearsing in Sam's front room for a couple of months, we thought we were getting quite good. So Sam bought a real guitar. I think it was a Fender Broadcaster, worth a small fortune now but a cheaper model back then. Griff got a set of Olympic drums, and I bought (on h.p.) a Hofner President bass.

The only downside to all of this was that Stan, the only one who could really play, had realised that Pongo couldn't sing or play anything, and the rest of us were, at best, below average. So he decided to leave. He joined a band that were all set up with proper gear and gigs at a local youth club in Nechells. They were called the Prospectors and were very good. Stan joined with an old friend of his who played drums, Lenny. They were going great guns, and then Stan and Lenny got the sack—can't remember why now, and neither can Stan. I can't ask Lenny, as he now lives in the United States. They then both joined another band called Monopoly. Louie Clark joined them soon after and later became one of the main men in ELO.

Stan went on to join Raymond Froggatt, a very well-known singer/songwriter and has made and is still making a good living out of music. I still see Stan now and then, mainly when he is gigging down in Cornwall. He changed his name many years ago to Hartley Caine, or H as most people call him. I can't say I blame him; Stan South is not really a name one would associate with a successful musician. I do sometimes forget and call him Stan, but he's OK with that—like I said, he is one of life's good guys. After all this time, H still maintains that he didn't leave the group; he says that he stayed, and we all left!

It was around this time that our so-called manager and photo man, Nelly, also decided to leave and went with Stan. We haven't seen him since. I tried to find him once, just for old times' sake. But when I actually found him, he said he didn't know me and slammed the door in my face! I seem to have that effect on people.

We needed to replace Stan, so we asked another old friend who used to be

4

a neighbour of Sam and Griff's, Tony. He could play guitar a little and had a background in music, having been in a school brass band with his brother, Ray. Also, we decided, for some silly reason, that all groups had to have a manager, and Tony's dad seemed the perfect person, as he had his own toolmaking company so knew about managing. Tony joined us, and before long he had a Fender Stratocaster in salmon pink. This was the guitar that any person who had any interest in playing in a group would have gladly killed for; it was the Rolls-Royce of guitars.

The other thing we needed was an amplifier to put these wonderful instruments through. We ended up with a Bird organ amp with four inputs. I can't for the life of me remember where we got it or who paid for it—probably Tony's dad—but we had an amp. Sam's front room was the place we still rehearsed with two guitars, a bass guitar, and a really cheap crystal mic, all going into this Bird amp. How it stayed in one piece I'll never know, but it was better than Sam's radiogram that we had been using! We were new to this kind of thing, and in our innocence, we decided that, because this Bird amp didn't have an earth wire (we found out later that it didn't need one), the safest way would be to give it one. So we ran a wire from the amp out of the window and stuck it in the ground! Health and safety, screw you!

The other thing that we needed was of course a name. Well, we must have gone through hundreds of them; even our parents were coming up with names. Some of them were beauts—the School Friends and the Great Barbarians. In the end, we thought that, because Griff had a lot of hats, we would call ourselves The Mad Hatters. Good or what?

Our favourite pastime around that time, apart from hanging around street corners, was watching other groups at various venues that were within walking distance. The two main ones were Brooklyn Farm Tech, which was about half a mile away, and the Beeches pub. Although we were underage, we always seemed to be able to get in one way or another. Brooklyn Farm Tech was on a Friday or Saturday night, and they had some really good bands on. The two that spring to mind are the Defenders and the Modenaires, both really good bands. They made you want to get to their level and play those kinds of gigs; and remember, we weren't playing any gigs at all. The Beeches pub was on our estate about five hundred yards away, so very handy. I think it was Sam's dad who used to get us in there, as he was a regular. The gigs there were on Sunday lunchtimes, and they would have some good bands on from all over the midlands, including the ones we would see at Brooklyn Farm. The one that stands out for me was Denny Laine and the Diplomats. Denny Laine went on to join the Moody Blues and, later, Wings.

We had, in our minds, reached the stage where we needed a gig. We had about four or five songs we could perform reasonably well and were getting nowhere in Sam's front room. So we got ourselves a spot at the Beeches Road School Friday night youth club. This was quite a big thing for us because we would quite often go to the youth club to watch the bands they had on.

Our favourite was The Little People. They were a very good band and had been on the TV on a pop program, so were quite well known locally. We knew most of the band—really nice blokes—Dave Potter, Roy Clifton, Keith Bailey, Micky Avery, and Micky Bishop. Griff and I used to spend hours just talking to Dave Potter about groups and gigs and everything to do with bands; we were very keen. Apart from Roy Clifton, who I still see quite regularly, I haven't seen any of the other members of the Little People for years. I know Micky Bishop lives in Spain, but the others are still living around the Midlands somewhere. Unfortunately, Dave Potter died recently, a great shame.

Anyway, the Friday we were to play came around, and we were really nervous, especially me. But we got there and set up our gear, which didn't take long, one Bird amp and the drums. We checked that everything worked and *waited. It was the most nervous I have ever been in my life. And when the time came to do our four numbers, I just couldn't go out there on stage in front of all my schoolmates, so I stood behind the curtains for the whole four numbers, hoping that no one would know it was me. Apparently, all you could see of me was the head of my guitar sticking out from behind the curtains. As it was, maybe that was a good thing because the gig was awful, a total failure. I don't think we were in tune; Pongo was drunk. and we didn't really know what we were doing. Good start or what! Back to the drawing board.*

You would think after an initiation like that most normal people would call it a day, but to say that we were normal is pushing it. We were still playing silly games, like hanging a bag of wet leaves in the tree outside Sam's house connected to a string that ran across the footpath. When someone walked down the street and caught the string with their feet, the bag of wet leaves would fall on their head. And of course, we would be watching from Sam's house and giggling like school kids. The other silly trick was to get Sam to go outside for something and then lock him out of his own house. On one occasion, he could see what we were going to do and ran down his path to try and get back in before we locked the door. He was a little bit late and couldn't stop and ended up putting his hand through the glass door. It was OK though; it didn't affect his playing. He's probably still got the scar.

Our next gig was at another school youth club, this time at the local comprehensive school, Great Barr Comp. We were going to be paid for this, so it had to be a lot better than the last one. We rehearsed like mad to try to get it right. And on the night, it was a little better but not much. I stood on the stage and not in the wings, which was a plus for me. We were in tune, just. And the numbers were not too bad.

The main problem that night was our wonderful singer. He was totally legless and couldn't remember the words or even the numbers and was staggering all over the place. I even think he missed his mouth when trying to play the gob iron, and to miss that mouth took some doing!

It went OK; all the kids thought, That's rock and roll. You have to remember that there were very few groups around at that time, and a lot of younger kids had never seen a live band; so even if you were bad (which we were), the kids thought it was great.

Well, we got paid, I think it was £2 our first paid gig. We spent it on fish and chips and a can of coke each and sacked Pongo.

I think it was to try and distance ourselves from the embarrassment of our dismal first gigs that we decided to change the name of the band. We thought we would go upmarket a bit and named our band Le Clique. We didn't know what it meant but thought it sounded good, so we set off one evening with a load of posters announcing that the Mad Hatters were now called Le Clique, and we stuck them anywhere and everywhere. I still like that name.

So now we had a few things to sort out—first to get a singer who could sing and next to rehearse like mad to try and get it to sound a lot better. Also, we needed some more gear. I managed to persuade my parents to sign for a half-decent bass and a Vox AC30 amp; Griff got a set of premier drums; and Sam, if I remember right, ended up with an AC30. I can't remember what guitar he had at that time, but I think it was still the Fender Esquire.

We found a great place to rehearse, the Clifton Cinema on Sunday mornings when it was closed. We knew the cleaning lady, and she let us in when she was cleaning. The only problem was it was about a mile from where Sam and Griff lived, and that's where all the gear was kept. When I say all the gear, it was very little really; we could fit it all in the back of Tony's dad's car, which we did on many occasions. But we had no choice, it was getting too much for Sam's front room, so we had to move to the cinema, and we had to get the gear there.

Sometimes we got lucky, and Bobby Baily, who lived opposite Griff would give us a lift—until we ripped his car seat with something, and that was the end of that. So we used a handcart borrowed from the scouts. We'd load everything onto this cart; it was like a cart you'd see being pulled by a horse, only smaller and being pulled by four young lads—up this bloody great hill that was Beeches Road. By the time we got there, we were knackered.

We also found a singer who could sing. His name was Tom Bridgewater, and he also went to the same school as Sam and me but was a year older. Having talked to everyone connected to the band, we still don't remember how we came to end up with Tom being our singer. I don't think anybody had any connection with him at school, him being that much older. However it happened, it happened. He had a good voice but not really the image; for example, he would turn up in jeans with a smart crease down the front. Tom was too neat really but a good singer and a good laugh. His parents were into ballroom dancing, and so was Tom. If you went to his house, you had to take your shoes off before they'd let you in, which was fine by us, as our shoes were normally covered in dirt from taking the shortcut to Tom's house across the fields.

After all this rehearsing, we were told we could do a little spot at the Beacon Cinema, (a sister cinema to the Clifton about a mile away) for the young kids at the Saturday morning matinee. It was the first time it had been done. You must remember that pop groups were really a new thing then, and not many people had seen a live group, so it was quite a big thing. We set all the gear up earlier and watched the first half of the matinee. Then in the break, as well as buying ice cream, we appeared on the stage and played about three or four numbers.

Well, if you have ever seen films of the Beatles being mobbed, that was what it was like. The kids went crazy. We were stuck outside on the steps of the cinema for ages just signing autographs. We thought, This is it; we've made it to the big time. The fact that they were 10-year-olds and didn't know a live band from a brown bear was not the point; it felt good.

I think it was that little taste of what could be that gave us a boost—and the fact that we all had jobs by then so were earning. Before long, we were getting much better gear around us. I bought a second-hand Fender Precision bass. (I wish I still had it; it would be worth a small fortune now.) Tony changed his guitar for a keyboard. We got a proper PA system, real mics. And things were going great. We started to do quite a few gigs, playing quite often at Calshot Road School and places like the Co-op Youth Club with the help of Mrs Waddop, who thought see knew all about groups and once told me to turn the bass down. Only she pronounced it bass as in the fish (sea bass); get it!

One gig that sticks in my mind was at some bowling club in Wednesbury. We arrived there early and set up the gear, so with time to spare we decided to play football on the Bowling Green. We were just about to start when the managers turned up and nearly had a fit; it was lucky they let us do the gig. Sam had this habit of standing with one foot on top of the other, which put him off balance. And on this night, he fell backwards, landing on the amps and the drums. Everything went everywhere; it was quite funny.

We were transported everywhere by Tony's dad or anyone else who had a car and was willing to help out. But as we got more gear it was becoming a problem, and we had to get a van. This was a Bedford Dormobile, pale blue with sliding doors that would fall off if you opened them too far and a three-speed column change gearbox. We thought it was the bee's knees.

It was kept at Griff's house, and one really cold day, it wouldn't start. Griff said it should start. 'I've put antifreeze in it.' It was a mystery until we found out that Griff had put the antifreeze in the petrol tank!

It was all very well having a van, but the problem was no one could drive. So we got our old friend Richard Lewis, Lou, another school friend from Beeches Road, to be our roadie. We even covered the van in messages in lipstick from 'fans'. We did quite a few gigs with that van.

At a gig we did in Bridgenorth, Lou was tired, so he went to sleep in the van while we did the gig. He was woken up by a few yobs, who didn't like the band or were jealous of the attention we were getting from the girls and had decided to turn the van over with Lou inside. Fortunately, they were chased off by Lou, who was pissed at being woken up.

Things like that happened quite regularly. We were at the Museum Pub in Sutton one night, and an almighty fight started—with chairs, tables, and mike stands all flying around the room. Again, we escaped unhurt.

We would spend our Saturdays visiting the music shops in Birmingham city centre. There were quite a few then, and we got to know the staff well. One shop was run by three members of a jazz band, the Jerry Allan Trio. They appeared on a lunchtime show on local TV everyday called Lunchbox, so we were mixing with the celebs already! In another shop there was a guy named Pete Oliver, who was a very good guitar player. He used to play his version of 'Daisy' for us. It was very funny because he used to play it slightly off. Sadly, he died in 2012.

We were starting to play with well-known groups at some of our gigs. One of the first was at the Plaza Handsworth. There, we supported the Fortunes, who at the time were at number one in the charts with 'You've Got Your Troubles.' They were a fantastic band and really nice blokes. We got to mix with these bands because we had to share a dressing room.

At the end of the night, we were outside trying to start our van when the Fortunes came out to get in their brand-new van. They ended up pushing our van down the road to start it!

Lou's time with us came to an end when we were playing at the Rainbow Room nightclub in Brum. We were supporting the Idle Race, who had a couple of minor hits. The singer and guitarist was Geoff Lynn, who was to become one of the biggest names in the pop world with ELO and the Traveling Wilburys, as well as being a prolific songwriter.

I still occasionally see a couple of the guys from the Idle Race, Dave and Greg at a club in Sutton Coldfield, along with another old friend and almost pop star, Mike Sheridan. Mike Sheridan was very well known in the Midlands and further afield as someone who really should have made the big time. But he didn't like to travel that much so couldn't be bothered. I played in Mike's band for a while and must say he is still probably one of the best frontmen I've ever seen. Sometimes Griff (who I tend to go to this club with) and I get called up to do a spot with Mike, our old boss.

Anyway, going back to the Rainbow Room. As I remember it, it was upstairs, and Lou didn't think we were helping enough to get the gear in. Anyway, we had a row, and he stormed off and went home on the bus, which left us with a van that none of us could drive. I think it ended up with me driving home, with everybody *chipping in on how to drive it. From then on, we drove the van ourselves, hoping that we didn't get stopped.*

As we all still had jobs, the number of gigs we were getting was getting very tiring. But that was to change. Griff was working at a jeweller's in the city, and I was working at W H Smiths about one hundred yards up the road from him. One day, Griff was called into the office and told he needed to get his hair cut or leave, so he left! About the same time, maybe a couple of days earlier, my boss had informed me I was to go on a training course to London for four days. As it clashed with a gig we had booked, I refused to go, and I got the sack. Told you we were keen!

We had a habit of stealing road signs and posters and sticking them on the inside wall of the van, a harmless little prank, until you get caught. Which we were! We foolishly parked in Brum on double yellow lines and came back to find the van had been towed away. No problem until you remember no one had a licence. I 'borrowed' Lou's licence to show the police when we went to pick up the van, and that was no problem. But then they wanted to know where all the signs had come from and pointed out the fact that the rear lights didn't work. And where had we gotten the roadworks' lamp that we'd hung on the back in place of the lights?

How we got away with it all is a total mystery. It must have been our stunning good looks and personality. But away with it we got, with the promise to put everything right. I don't think Tony's dad was impressed, being as it was him who'd insured the van.

The old van was not in very good shape really. Apart from the doors falling off, the column change gearstick fell off, and we had to change gear with a pair of mole grips clamped on to the column. But the worst was when we were driving past Birmingham Airport going to Coventry when the brakes failed; we ended up flying around the island and into a layby.

I believe it was soon after that we upgraded to a Ford Thames van that we got from a school. It had previously been a camper, so had a sunroof. There were various things that we had to change, but the sunroof stayed—unfortunately, as it leaked!

I later took my driving test in that van and failed—not, I hasten to add, because my driving was bad, but because the passenger seat, which was not bolted down, used to move backwards and forwards on its runners. This suited us, as it made it easier to climb in and out when the side door jammed. But anyway, on my driving test, all was going well until the examiner told me to do an emergency stop. Well, the van stopped, but the examiner didn't. He went shooting forwards into the windscreen. I think the fact that I couldn't stop laughing didn't help.

I later took my test in John Park's Vauxhall 101 and passed. So there! Johnny Parks was one of our friends who we sometimes called upon to help us out with various problems we would have, such as driving the van or helping shift gear here or there.

We were, by now, getting good and wanted to move along. We were doing covers of the charts and getting a bit of a fan base. So we decided to enter a competition at the Silver Blades Ice Rink, a popular spot in Brum that had well-known groups on a regular basis. Thus, we thought it would be nice to play there anyway. The prize was £100, a mini tour of the other ice rinks around the country, and a recording test for EMI. Got to be worth a go, right!

After a couple of heats of the competition, we were still in it; in fact, we got through to the final. We got ourselves a uniform so that we looked the part and rehearsed the number we were going to play in the final. It was a number by the Yardbirds called 'For Your Love'.

Well, we won! How about that! I think Tony got the prize for best keyboard player, and I got the prize for best bass player (just shows what the standard must have been like). It was, as I remember, a little medal.

The test for EMI was arranged for the following month, I believe. We went down to London the day before, the reason being that we'd heard a new supergroup had been formed and were playing at a youth club in Middlesex the night before our recording. So off we went.

We couldn't afford to stay in a hotel, so we took a load of camping gear, borrowed from the local scout troop. We camped out on a common. It could have been Clapham Common, but I'm not sure.

The band in question was Cream, and what a band they were—fantastic. The club was very small, so we were really up close and personnel. As for our recording, it went quite well. It was at Abbey Road Studios. And, yes, we did walk across the zebra crossing, but we had to go into the studio normally used for orchestras, as the others were in use. Our problem was that we never had any original material so recorded a couple of covers. They were OK but nothing special. I think there are still a couple of copies knocking around somewhere. It didn't bring us the fame and fortune we were aiming for but was a great experience.

We did our little mini tour of the ice rinks that was part of our prize; it gave us I suppose our first taste of playing outside the Midlands as we did Bristol, Sheffield, Manchester, and so on. We also played the ice rink where we'd won the competition, the Silver Blades in Brum. It was quite exciting, as we were to be the support act for one of the biggest bands around, who had had hit records singing about bus stops and siblings who ain't too heavy, if you get my drift.

When we arrived at the ice rink, we asked the manager which dressing room to use, as there were two. We were told to use either one, as they were both the same. So we chose one and put our clothes and stuff in there. We were to open the show as support so got into our stage gear, ready to go.

It was then that Alan Smith the singer with this band came into our dressing room and told us to get out because this was their dressing room. We told him that they were both the same and that they should use the one next door. But he became quite abusive, saying they wanted this dressing room and that they were the stars and so on and so forth. After a few choice words, on our part mainly, they used the other dressing room. It was, I have to say, one of the few occasions where the big-name acts acted like tossers.

After our little mini tour, we thought about changing the line-up of the band. Things were changing, and soul was becoming very popular. So we decided to add some brass and turn it from a pop band to a soul band. I must say, it was by a majority vote, and some were not particularly happy about it but went along with it. We asked Ray, Tony's brother, to join—he played trumpet—and Tom's friend Mick. Mick said he had a sax and, although he had only just started to play, was keen to learn and join the band.

Mick was older than the rest of us by about two years so more mature—or so you would have thought. Not so; he was worse than us. He used to delight in saying the obvious, and when you pointed it out, he would roar with laughter. He called them 'chokers'. Strange man. His pride and joy at the time was his car. It was an A35 van with windows in the side, but the thing that he thought was special was that it had a rear windscreen wiper! Like I said, a strange man. No one has seen him for years.

So now we were a seven-piece band playing soul music. We spent a lot of time rehearsing and finally got it about right—well, almost! We thought that the new band should have a new name, so we changed our name once again. This time we were called Whiskey Mac. It would be the last time we changed the name.

We were getting quite busy now and doing a couple of gigs a week. We played a lot at the Plaza in Handsworth. It was a good place to play because they had all the top bands of the day there, and we got to meet them. We played with quite a few—the Fortunes; Dave Berry; Duane Eddy (a big, big star but the shyest man

*you'd ever meet, who rarely, if ever, looked at his audience and never said a word);
Crispian St. Peters; and the Drifters. We worked with the Drifters quite a lot,
and they had different members nearly every time.*

*We didn't earn a lot at the Plaza, but it was great fun. There were always at
least two bands on, and when the big names were there, you had three bands—
two support and the main attraction. The owner of the Plaza was a Mrs Reagan.
She owned three clubs—the Plaza Handsworth, Plaza Old Hill, and the Ritz
in Kings Heath. Sometimes you would do a double for her or even do the three
clubs in one night. That was a nightmare, trying to get your gear packed away
and then trying to set up at the other end. But it was a great learning process and
a good laugh at times.*

*We once played at the Plaza Old Hill with a local band, the Exception, a
very good band whose bass player, Dave Pegg, went on to play with Jethro Tull
and, later, Fairport Convention.*

*We played with a band who had just had a massive hit singing about Eddy
Cochran. The singer used to play with a band who had a hit about a satellite that
finally fell to earth in the sixties. Well, everyone had to share a dressing room. But
they wanted it all to themselves so got the manager to turf us all out. It turns out
that they were probably the worst band we had ever seen, so the night ended with
us and the Exception watching this band with amusement.*

*Another night, Mrs Reagan asked us to back a well-known singer, as his band
hadn't turned up. So with no rehearsal, we just had to get on and do it. What a
farce that turned out to be.*

*Old Ma Reagan, as she was called (but only behind her back), wouldn't let
you take any guest into the venues only your spouses. So all of our girlfriends had
curtain rings on their fingers.*

Things like having to stand in for other bands and trying to get your girlfriend into the gigs happened now and again. We were working for a couple of different agencies at the time, one being a well-known agency in Wolverhampton, and we did quite a lot of work for them. They booked us for a gig, somewhere in Wolverhampton I think, supporting a quite heavy group, who were known at the time.

We arrived, set up, and waited for the stars of the show to turn up. They didn't and wouldn't. We were told we would have to go on as them, who played a totally different type of music. How they thought we'd get away with it … well, we didn't. After about two or three numbers, most of the crowd had gone home. We must have given them a great 'rep'.

The same agency also used to book a local band who were very popular, Slade, or as they were then called, Ambrose Slade. They were a very good band. We worked with them a couple of times in a pub in Wolverhampton called the Star and Garter. There was a big room upstairs where bands performed every week.

I remember doing bonfire night there with them. It went well, and we all had a good night. After we had packed the gear away, our van wouldn't start—nothing new there then. And Slade, being the good guys they were, helped us push the van around the car park to get it to start. Unfortunately, it started backfiring, which, considering it was 1.30 in the morning, was not a good thing. It wasn't long before a neighbour shouted out of his bedroom window to 'shut the f*** up', thinking we were setting off fireworks.

This was understandable, but not to one of the band, who yelled back at the guy and even offered him out!

We met some really nice people on our travels; one of the nicest was Terry Sylvester. We were playing at Molineaux football ground, Wolverhampton Wanderers if you didn't know, playing support to the Swinging Blue Jeans, and Terry was the guitar player. He had recently joined them from the Escorts, a very *good Liverpool band that never really got the credit they deserved. Anyway, he liked our band, and we spent most of the night deep in conversation about bands and music and the music business in general. He was a really nice bloke, and we were glad when we heard he'd made the big time and joined our 'favourite' band—who we'd supported at the ice rink and had the disagreement with over dressing rooms. At least now there was one really nice person in that band.*

We also met Roy Orbison around this time. When I say we met Roy Orbison, we didn't actually meet him. But we did pass within six inches of him as we were going into the Connaught Hotel in Coventry and he was coming out—so another 'almost' you could say.

Around this time, we played a charity gig at Calshot Road School to raise money for kidney disease. We decided to do this because a friend of the band, John Doyle, who lived a couple of doors from Sam, had kidney disease and sadly lost his fight for life. And Griff had also lost his brother, Robert to the same disease. This was advertised in the local paper, and we managed to raise quite a lot for the charity.

Chapter 2

Whiskey Mac

I think our time at Abbey Road gave us a taste for recording. Although I personally hated it and still do, it was the only way to achieve our goal. So, with that in mind, we went to a recording studio in Northfield run by Jimmy Powell for Strike Records. Jimmy had had a top ten hit in the early sixties with a song called 'Sugar Baby', and Strike Records also had a record in the charts with Lou Christie called 'Lightning Strikes', so it seemed as good a place as any.

Jimmy claimed that he'd discovered Rod Stewart—said he found him in London and gave him a job in his band, the Dimensions. I think Rod Stewart must have outshone Jimmy, because he sacked him within a couple of months.

We recorded a couple of songs at the Strike studio, but one that stands out was written by Jimmy and called 'Walking through the Night'. We recorded it a couple of times, and it was really very good. We all thought that, with the right backing, it could have done something. But that's where money comes into play. We didn't have any, and neither did Jimmy.

To say Jimmy was a character was an understatement. He was also a bit of a nutter. We would be recording in the studio, doing our best, and he would be joking around with some girl in the control room. If his wife had walked in, she wouldn't have been very pleased. She knew about his ways and accepted it but sometimes, so he told us, she made him sleep on his own. I think that if we hadn't have been there on occasions, he would probably be dead (not really). She used to tell him not to go to sleep or she would just keep waking him up. Can't say as I blame her; he was a bit of a joker.

Jimmy was a great singer and frontman, and we were really chuffed when he asked us to be his backing band with the Dimensions for an upcoming tour of the universities. We rehearsed until we were ready, and off we went. The first uni we did was Nottingham, where we were billed alongside the Scaffold ('Lily the Pink' and so on). There was another band, but I can't remember who it was. It went really well, and we all had a good time as far as I remember (I think the drink was kicking in about now).

We then did Birmingham, Newcastle, and Lancaster, where Jimmy didn't turn up at all. He was often late getting to gigs. He used to travel with his manager in his car—no common van for our Jimmy. But that was the first time he failed to turn up. You can imagine the scene, Jimmy Powell and the Dimensions, without Jimmy Powell. Chaos reigned yet again. The best of that was that we still paid him!

All this time we were travelling to these gigs in the van—and there weren't that many motorways then, remember—a van that had no heater, a sunroof that leaked, and windscreen wipers that only worked sometimes. When the windscreen wipers didn't work, we tied shoelaces to the wiper blades and put one end in the driver's window and the other end in the passenger's window and pulled them.

Tom often used to travel in his car, a Ford pop sit up and beg. He was the only one to own a car, unless you count Griff's 1947 Rover that never went farther than the end of the gully at the back of his house. The reason Tom travelled in his car was so that he could pick Ray up from school and shoot straight to that night's gig.

I remember going with Tom to a gig in Manchester, and the car broke down. We had to hire a car to get to the gig—no money that night. Durham Uni was a particularly good gig; we were billed with Geno Washington and the Ram Jam Band, Chris Farlow and the Thunderbirds, and Gary Farr and the T Bones, which included Keith Emerson. It was a great night.

These uni gigs were always good, and they always laid on food and drink and other things you wanted in your dressing room, which was a big bonus for us, as we didn't have to pay for it. At Durham there was a bowl of lychees in syrup in our dressing room. Never having seen them before, let alone tasted them, we didn't really like them. So they ended up being thrown around the room in a food fight that left us and the dressing room covered in lychees and syrup and assorted sandwiches. The uni staff were not impressed. But that's rock and roll!

We had a very similar experience a year or so later when we played Tewkesbury Town Hall with Amen Corner. We had to share a dressing room, but it was very difficult to get in or out of the dressing room because of the crowd of fans outside the door all screaming for the singer, Andy Fairweather Low. At one end of the room was a partition about six feet high, and Andy decided to climb over to see if there was another way out. He didn't find another way out, but he did find an enormous stash of booze, which he passed over to the rest of us. It didn't take long for us all to be pretty well out of it and covered in booze that was being thrown around; it must have smelt like a brewery. Both bands managed to do our spots, a lot worse for wear. God knows what it must have sounded like; we had trouble standing up, let alone playing. I don't think it made any difference because you couldn't hear anything for the screaming.

We worked with Jimmy for a few months and then left him and went on our merry way but not before we met his soon to be new backing band. We went into the studios a couple of weeks after we gave up our Dimension duties and met up with a band that had come down from up north to record. They were a nice bunch of lads with very strong accents who were recording a Motown song called 'Going to a Go-Go'. But the way they sang it, it was 'Goin t' Go-Go'. We were to meet up again in Hamburg when we played the same club for a couple of weeks with them and Jimmy Powell.

After we parted company with Jimmy, we carried on working for various agents, and we had a lot of work on. A gig that Sylvie, my then girlfriend and now wife of forty plus years, will remember was a New Year's Eve gig that we did at the Cofton Country Club at Rednal. We played with the Nashville Teens, who we worked with again later at Wolverhampton Civic Hall. Anyway, this New Year's Eve, it was snowing, and to get out of the car park meant driving up a quite steep incline to reach the road. Even with the weight of the equipment, the van couldn't do it. The only way was to push, so we all started to push the thing, including Sylvie. We got only so far, and the van started to slide back down the hill at about the same time as Sylvie slipped on the ice and into the path of the sliding van. Luckily, she managed to pull her legs out of the way before it ran over her.

The gig that I remember most was in Kidderminster, at a venue called Frank Freeman's Dancing Club. We thought that this would be an important gig because it seemed that the right people could be there. But it nearly didn't happen, as Griff and the roadie had been to Glasgow to watch a rugby match or some such thing but they were unexpectedly held up and had to spend another night there. They arrived back with hours to spare, and we did the gig.

They were all-nighters at Frank Freemans, normally 7 p.m. to 7 a.m. All-nighters seemed to be the in thing back then; lots of venues put them on. When you did an all-nighter at Franks, you played with another band, one hour on, one hour off, and so on. When we played gigs there, we worked with Robert Plant and the Band of Joy, who we also played Birmingham Uni with later in the year.

Robert Plant later found super stardom with Led Zeppelin. He was and still is a very nice guy. Sylvie and I were in the Manor House, a pub in West Bromwich, a few years later. Robert Plant came in with his wife/girlfriend, and, being a 'pop star', was getting all the looks. Having only met him a couple of times and not wanting to make a fool of myself, I thought I wouldn't say hello. But to my surprise he came over and said hello and talked about Frank Freemans. I must say it made my day, especially as everyone was watching, thinking, He knows Robert Plant.

All this time we were still travelling in the old Ford Thames, which had seen better days. To start it, we had to feel under the dash and hold two wires together, which was OK until we were stopped by the police, which was pretty regular. They asked the normal questions—drugs and the like—and told us to go, which is not that easy when you have to feel around under the dash trying to find the right wires while a policeman is standing there watching you. Luckily, we were very good at it.

We had done a couple of gigs at a nightclub in Birmingham called the Cedar Club; it was very well known and probably the best club in town. We were very pleased when the boss asked us to be one of the resident bands. It was quite a feather in our caps. The other resident band was called Wellington Kitch, also known as the Cedar Set. They were very good.

Tom, our singer, who had a good job with an insurance company, decided that the band was getting too much work and taking up too much time; I'll never know how he managed to combine the two. Now, he told us that he was leaving.

On the Beeches Estate, where we still all lived, there were a number of groups; as I said before, groups were all over the place. One of the most popular was a group called the Cinnette Sounds. They were not like us; they were more a pop band and did a lot of weddings and parties. The singer was a very nice guy, Alan, a teacher who we all knew. He seemed to fit in with our weird sense of humour, and he loved the kind of music we were playing. As a bonus, he could sing! So we stole him, kind of a free transfer.

It worked out very well, and Alan got thrown in the deep end by working the Cedar Club on a regular basis, a club that most of the local bands would have given their high teeth to play. The club attracted a lot of minor celebs, among them Johnny Prescott, a well-known boxer, and Pat Roach, a wrestler who appeared on a TV wrestling show quite often. Pat Roach was always the gentle giant—a very nice man. He would sit at the bar and talk to anyone. If there was any trouble, he would act as the unofficial bouncer, along with the official ones. But I never saw him hit anyone. He would pick them up above his head, take them to the front door, put them down on the pavement. and tell them to go (in no uncertain terms).

A number of top acts also played the Cedar Club including the Move, the Drifters, and a few others that I can't remember. Because we were there quite often, we got to know the bar staff very well, and although drinks in the club where very expensive, we always managed to drink a lot at very little cost. One of the bosses of the club was rumoured to have links with the criminal underworld. How true that was, we'll never know, but they were always all right with us. Unfortunately, the Cedar Club no longer exists.

We were doing a lot of work for an agency in Birmingham called Intercity Agencies, and our contact there was a guy named John Tanner, a prat but a good agent. We were Tanner's favourite band, probably because we earned him the most money, but for whatever reason, he took us under his wing and became our manager. Tanner got us so much work it was sometimes hard to keep up; we were all over the place.

The problem was, he didn't think of the logistics—just the gigs and the money. For example, a double, two gigs on the same night, was OK if they were close to each other. But when they are 120 miles apart, it can become a problem.

He once gave us Redcar and Bradford. We got to Redcar to find we were playing with another band and that they had put us on last. We had to see the management and get them to change it around so that we could get away early enough to get to Bradford. While we were waiting to go on, we played football on the beach. After the Redcar gig we had to pack away asap—thank God for roadies—and hit the road. The gig in Bradford was an all-nighter, so we thought we would be OK. Unfortunately, John the roadie, with our help, got lost, and we didn't get to the Bradford gig until about 4 a.m., just about the time most of the punters were going home. So we played the set to an almost empty club.

The thing I remember about that trip was sleeping on top of the gear in the back of the van and falling off every time we went round a corner. But that was the kind of gig we were getting from Mr Tanner. He got us a regular gig at a pub in Sutton-in-Ashfield near Nottingham on Wednesday nights. It wasn't too far, but the drawback was they wanted us there by 6.30. As we had to pick Ray up from school at 4, we never got there before 7.30; so it was always a rush. The pub boss was not happy, but it was regular work.

We were booked to do a weekend in Cornwall, starting in Bude and ending in Plymouth. On the way down, and remember it was before all the motorways, we pulled into a layby. The farmer had put a sign on the gate to his field saying, 'This is not a toilet. Please don't urinate here.' Well, we thought that would look good on the back of the van. So we tied the sign to the back door, which amused the people who followed us. It didn't amuse the police though, and they stopped us, made us take it off, and threatened to charge us with theft. Once again, we talked our way out of it; we were getting good at that.

We did the Bude gig, a large hall right on the seafront. The manager told us we could sleep in his office above the hall, which was good, because we, as normal, had no money for hotels; and it made a change from sleeping in the van, which we did most of the time. We even slept in the van for two nights when we did some of the big nightclubs in London—fame, eh.

When we got to Plymouth, we went to see Birmingham City play Plymouth Argyle, us being City supporters. On the way back from Plymouth, the weather turned nasty; it rained really hard and was very cold. The heater in the van didn't work, and with the leaking sunroof, we were cold and wet and took it in turns to sit on the engine cover. But whoever's turn it was to sit there had a very hot ass. After a few miles, the engine started to overheat, which meant the van also filled with steam. But at least the steam was warm. It was the most miserable trip ever, and it took us about eight hours. We must get another van!

I think the last gig with the old van was in Leeds at a club called the Spinning Disc. It was a really good night, and as normal, we were going to sleep in the van, as we were gigging in Tadcaster the next night. I'm not sure who it was, me or Ray I think, but we got talking to a girl, as one does, and we went back to her house. Her parents were away, so we spent the night—all seven of the band and the girl—in a double bed, cosy. But apart from sleep, which we never seemed to get enough of, nothing happened—amazing! We left the roadie to sleep in the van.

After that episode, the Tadcaster gig was quite boring. I think at that time we had Dave Birtwhistle helping out as roadie, which could be quite difficult. At a gig at the Imperial Ballroom in Burnley, there was a revolving stage, but the PA speakers had to stay on the sides of the stage, the part that didn't revolve, which meant that, as soon as we finished the set, the stage started to turn, and Bert had to run like a maniac to unplug the speakers from the PA amp that turned with us. He just about made it.

A few weeks later, we borrowed the money from Tony's dad and bought a long-wheelbase Transit van. It had a heater that worked; no leaks; wipers; and proper seats, front and back. Luxury, pure luxury!

We were getting more and more work with John Tanner. We were doing three- and four-day tours in Yorkshire and Cumbria. I remember on one such trip getting stopped on the M1 by the police, who said they had received reports from lorry drivers of being shot at from a passing van. The policeman opened the door of the van, and a load of dried peas fell down onto his shoes.

'Peas is it? We were told it was gravel.'

What had happened was that, on the way through a town, we had stopped for something to eat and seen a toy shop. Well, being the big boys that we were, we bought pea-shooters and peas and thought it funny to shoot at lorries as we passed them on the motorway.

The police were not happy and when they looked inside the van they pointed to Mick and said, 'You look the oldest. You should have more sense.'

To this, Ray replied, 'He has. he's got a water pistol.'

The copper turned to the roadie and told him that he was in charge of the vehicle and as such he was responsible for the safety of the vehicle and passengers, the roadie said he was only doing what he was told to do by his employers, which was true. I was charged with a minor offence (peashooter) and pleaded guilty and fined.

John the roadie I'm talking about was John Cheadle. John was our main roadie for quite a long time. He too was an old friend from the Beeches and was the only one out of all our friends who had a decent car. From what I can remember, it was a Ford Anglia 1200cc that he had souped up with bigger wheels and a bigger engine. It looked really good.

We had a number of roadies so it could have been any one of them but the roadie would pass a milk float and I would take a bottle of milk for breakfast.

Our roadie left us not long after that and joined another local band called Orange Garden, who were about to go off to Germany. It was a great shame *because we all got on well, but we all remain friends to this day. He now lives in Spain for most of the year, only coming back in the summer months when it's too hot down there. It's a hard life for some!*

It was all getting too much for Sam, with him still working and trying to make a career for himself. So he left the band. It was sad because, apart from being a good friend, he was one of the founding members. I think Sam's leaving affected Tony more than anyone; he had been close to Sam for many years, and his departure, I think, made Tony think about the band.

Once again, we raided another local band, the aforementioned Orange Garden, nicking Dave Toy, one of the best guitar players around at that time and very experienced. The band had just returned from Germany, and I think that living together in Germany and all the travelling had caused problems within the band, so we jumped in. Dave fitted in great with us all and gave us a lift we needed about then.

The band had always seemed to be in two teams, if you like, and was competitive. There was a time when, if you got a girl into the back of the van at a gig, you got a notch on your side of the van roof for your team. I, of course, had nothing to do with this practice!

John Tanner very often came to gigs with us, and it could be quite embarrassing at times. We would walk into a venue and meet with the promoter, and Tanner would be telling him, 'My band don't do support slots; they go on last or not at all' and so on and so forth. Or before you got to the venue, he'd say, 'When we get there, talk with a London accent, as I've billed you from London.' Or it would be a Liverpool accent if he'd billed us from Liverpool.

Having said that, he did get us a lot of good gigs. This included gigs in Glasgow and in London at the Whiskey A Go Go and the Pink Flamingo and the like. It was in London before we did the gig at the Pink Flamingo that we decided to get a uniform; it seemed the thing to do. So we went to a clothes shop in Wardour Street just down the street from the Pink Flamingo and bought black trousers and red shirts with big frills down the front, very chic.

I think that must have been the start of my hatred of wearing uniforms in bands. They looked OK in some places, but in others, they were just an embarrassment.

We did a couple of gigs in Glasgow at the Mecca Ballroom, I think. And remember that Glasgow was a lot rougher then. They still had the big tenement blocks and lots of dock workers. Anyway, were doing the gig and eyeing the girls— well the ones without the tattoos and nose rings (mind you, Mick liked all that kind of stuff, weird man)—when a big guy got up on stage and asked me what size shoes I took.

I said size 8.

And he said, 'Well step on that, ya b*****,' throwing his fag on the floor.

Now that anywhere else would have been funny. But when you're outnumbered about 200 to 1 in Glasgow, believe me, it's not. And I think the frilly shirts had a lot to answer for at that gig.

A gig in Norwich was interesting, as above the stage of this very big nightclub were cages containing quite scantily clad dancing girls, which was very nice but quite a distraction. You were forever looking up; it's a wonder no one fell off the stage.

One of Tanner's more unsuccessful ventures was a tour we did backing Jerry Conley, brother of Arthur Conley, of 'Sweet Soul Music' fame, trying to cash in on his brother's name. The truth was Jerry was really a labourer from Bilston, and the only thing he had going for him was that his American accent was good! That 'tour' didn't last long. On one of these gigs the 'star' didn't turn up. We got through the gig OK, and the venue manager paid us instead of Tanner. Tanner *was there and wanted the money. We said we wanted more because of the no-show. And Griff, who had the money, hid in the back of the van until Tanner gave up and went home. This was one of the rare occasions we won.*

On an earlier gig with Tanner—I think it was in Bristol or somewhere down that way—we decided to give him a bit of a fright. Years earlier, we were taken to a place called Whitley Court, which was near Kidderminster; it was an old manor house that had burnt down years before so that just a shell was left. In its day, it was quite a place and was used by the highest in the land, including royalty, Queen Victoria's son, the playboy prince, used the place as a retreat to meet his lady friends (or so rumour has it).

Anyway, this place was very spooky to say the least, and there was a church on the same site that was downright scary. On this particular night, we told Tanner we would take him somewhere interesting after the gig and told the roadies to go off first and set it all up. Off they went in the van, and we followed in the cars we used sometimes. By the time we got there with Tanner, it was about 3 a.m. and very dark.

We'd told Tanner we were taking him to a haunted house. The roadies had taken the covers off the PA speakers that were about five feet tall and turned them inside out so that they were white. We stayed with Tanner by the fence that was supposed to keep you out and just looked at the silhouette of the manor against the moon—perfect. Then the roadies began walking across the front of the manor about 50 yards away.

It worked a treat; all you could see was these white shapes that seemed to float about a foot above the ground. Even we were starting to doubt that these were our boys. It worked so well that Tanner even phoned the Melody Maker magazine and told them all about these ghosts he'd seen. And once it had appeared in the MM, it was too late to tell him the truth, especially as a member of the Spencer Davis Group wrote in the MM that he'd seen the ghosts as well.

There was a time when it looked as if Mick, our 'wonderful' sax player, might end up as an actual ghost. We were playing at a music festival at Cannon Hill Park in Birmingham along with the Mersey Beats when Mick began to feel ill and then collapsed. We took him to the medical tent, and they sent for an ambulance. Poor old Mick had a collapsed lung. Too much blowing!

Our time with John Tanner was at an end. He'd done us a lot of good and got us a lot of work, but he'd also caused us a lot of grief and owed us a lot of money. Or as he'd say, we'd been knocked! Griff and Alan used to see him at Birmingham football club and got on with him fine. Personally, I wouldn't want to speak to him. He owes us too much money.

We signed with a big agency in London, who also managed the Walker Brothers and a few other named bands. One of the first things the agency wanted us to do was to go to Germany. Tony was not at all keen and said that, if we decided to go, he would have to leave because of his commitment to his father's company. We decided we had to go for it. So unfortunately, Tony left.

Once again, we had to find a band member. And because Orange Garden had all but finished and were in the process of reforming with different members, we went along to one of their rehearsals and asked Phil Tree if he would join us as a keyboard player (he's one of those people who can play most things, bastard!) and come with us to Germany. Fortunately, he agreed so we were a full band once again.

But only because Griff was not too well at the time and was unsure if he would make Germany, he even asked the drummer from Orange Garden if he wanted to take his place. Luck must have been with us that day because he said no. so *Griff* had to go. And so a couple of weeks later, we were off to Germany. It may not seem a big thing now, but then it was the first time that most of us had been abroad.

Final line up off to Germany

Chapter 3

Flensburg

And so on to our German adventure but not quite. First, we had three major obstacles to overcome:

1. *Time. We didn't have any.*
2. *Money. We didn't have any.*
3. *Passports. We didn't have any.*

Time

Our management had contracted us to the German club for four weeks starting the following week. We were to be paid £800, which was not too bad when you consider that you could get a gallon of petrol for 40p and a packet of fags for 10p. The problem was, How do we get everything sorted and get there in a week?

Money

We were told by our management that the club we were working in would have accommodation and would pay us weekly in advance. But we still had the problem of getting enough money together for the ferry fare and petrol to get there.

Passports

We didn't have enough time to apply for passports. Nor did we have the money to pay for them. So we all went to the post office and got six-month visitor's passports for £1.

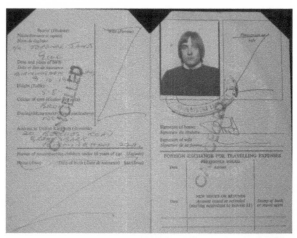

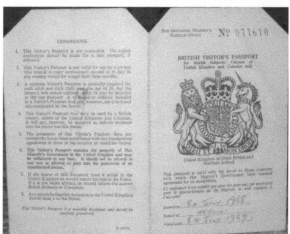

My first passport

Dave and Phil were OK because they had passports, having just come back from Germany with Orange Garden.

So problem 3, the passports, was sorted. Now on to problem 2. Well, most of us had to borrow money off friends or family. I borrowed money from Sylvie, who was the only person I knew who had any money anyway, which was amazing considering we had agreed to split up.

That left us with problem 1, time. Our destination in Germany was a town in the north called Flensburg. It was very close to the Danish border, which meant that the drive from Zeebrugge would be about twelve or thirteen hours. It would have been a lot quicker to get the ferry to Hamburg, which was only a couple of hours' drive to Flensburg. But we couldn't afford the fare, as it was far more expensive than the Dover to Zeebrugge ferry.

If I remember rightly, we arrived a day late—not too bad. But that increased the money problems because when we arrived at the club in Flensburg, they didn't know anything about accommodation or the weekly pay. As it was, the manager put us up in his house, in the loft. It was the first time we had ever seen duvets. We thought you had to get inside them. It must have been some sight, seeing seven blokes trying to climb inside the duvets. I think Mick managed it but couldn't get out again. We managed to get a sub off the owner and bought some food (our first for a while) and ended up living mainly off packet soup, bratwursts, and black bread, which is vile.

Anyway, I digress.

We set off for Dover, with a broken Transit, seven blokes, all the equipment, visitors' passports, a bit of food Ray's mother had given him, and no money. Hang on. Let's backtrack. Broken Transit—where did that come from? Well, we'd had our Transit for about two to three months. It had never really run that well, and it was quite heavy on fuel. But then, compared to what we'd had previously, it was still good, so we classed it as broken. We went on the ferry to Zeebrugge and just hoped that we had enough money for the fuel to get us the six hundred miles to Flensburg.

Somewhere on the way—we were in Germany by this time—we were pulled over by the police for speeding (we must have been going downhill). It was our first encounter with the German police but, unfortunately, not our last. In Germany at that time, you paid a statutory on-the-spot fine for speeding. I think it was the equivalent of about £5 to £10. Unfortunately, we didn't have that amount of money between us. (How sad is that?) The policeman didn't believe us, and it ended up with him waving his pistol around threatening to shoot us all. Fortunately, he didn't and let us off.

When we finally arrived in Flensburg, we found the club was a Western type of club called the Crazy Horse Saloon. It was on the front of a small harbour that never seemed to be used. I always remember coming out of the club in the small hours and seeing the harbour full of jellyfish; it was always full of jellyfish.

The best thing about the club was the football machine. We used to play the bar staff, who taught us how to play properly. We used to spend a lot of our spare time on that football machine.

Flensburg Harbour

When we started working at the club that night, there weren't many people in, and the boss told us to turn up the volume so that people passing knew there was a band playing. The trouble was, as soon as the punters started coming in, he would yell at us to turn it down. We couldn't win!

Ray was only 16 and shouldn't have been there in the first place. But he was very prone to falling in love with any girl he fancied, and it was in Flensburg that he fell in love with his first German girl. Her name was Karen. She was a very nice-looking girl as I remember but very friendly with most men, if you know what I mean. Ray used to take her out to the van every time we had a break from playing, normally about fifteen minutes. We didn't think it got much further than a quick grope and slap and tickle because he proudly announced that he lost his cherry later that year when we were in Hamburg. He used to make us laugh though because he would come back on stage and tell us, in detail, everything they had done together in the van. He even told us that he couldn't understand why Karen had a plaster on her arse—pox jab?

At the same time, I got quite friendly with the barmaid, Heidi. She used to come to the house and help make our meals, if you could call them that. Again, it was nothing serious—a bit of this and that. But I think she fell for my boyish charms (I'm wonderful). I was very chuffed about that because she was the best-looking girl in the place. Mind you, it was quite a seedy place anyway, but she was quite a looker. All the boys fancied her and really tried hard to chat her up, whereas I didn't think I had a chance so didn't bother at all; that was probably the reason I got lucky.

She said one day that she would take me somewhere special and came to pick me up one Sunday afternoon and off we went. The somewhere special turned out to be her house to meet her parents! What could I do? I sat there not knowing what to say, and if I'd have known what to say, I couldn't have said it. Her parents didn't speak English, and I couldn't speak German, so everything went via Heidi. I remember sitting there watching Bonanza, a Western, in German—very strange. It turned out her father was a policeman, which didn't help, and he also didn't like the English, especially me, a long-haired groupie. No wonder he was quiet.

We were booked for four weeks. But after, I think it was three weeks, we were told we had to go and see the immigration people. We didn't have work permits, only visitor passports that you weren't allowed to work on; and at 16, Ray was too young to work anyway. We were told we would have to stop working or leave Germany straight away. We stopped working and were kicked out of the club and, more importantly, out of our digs. So we had no work; nowhere to sleep, apart from the van; and no money because the club boss said that we had broken the contract we had with him, and therefore, he didn't have to pay us. I think in the end he gave us enough money to pay for petrol, but that was it.

We decided to go down to Hamburg, which was only about one hundred miles away and not too far off our route home. Dave and Phil had been to Hamburg before and knew a few people there, so we went to visit and stayed for three or four days. We all slept in the van outside the British Consulate. I think we stayed there because St Pauli, where all the clubs were, was a very rough area; we didn't fancy having the van broken into, especially if we were in it!

The people Dave and Phil knew all hung around the Star Club and the Top Ten Club on the Reeperbahn, the main street in St Pauli, not far from the docks. It was a useful few days, because, through Dave and Phil's friends, we meet the boss of the Top Ten Club. All the clubs around the area used UK groups, mainly because the German groups at the time were not too good; in fact, crap was a good word for them. The two best clubs in St Pauli were the Star Club and The Top Ten, so we were lucky to get an intro. We had a look around and met some of Phil and Dave's friends before going back to Birmingham.

42

Unfortunately, when we arrived back at Dover, we were stopped by customs and had the van searched from top to bottom looking for drugs. After all, we were a pop group, and as far as customs were concerned, all pop groups had drugs.

We were only in Brum for the day, as the day after we arrived back, we went to Peterborough to get proper passports. And two weeks later we were back in Germany! How our girlfriends must have loved us!

Chapter 4

Baumholder

Our next trip to the Fatherland was to a place called Baumholder. Never heard of it? Neither had we, but then we'd never heard of Flensburg, and we found that! Anyway, for your information, it's not too far from Frankfurt, and even we had heard of that. The trip to Flensburg had been a nightmare. Not only had it been six hundred miles in a van full of adult children (us), it had also been full of smelly farting adult children. Mick was probably the worst, mainly because he was always eating curry.

The main problem with the trip was the fact that the van, our almost new Transit, was not running right. It would get to about 60 mph, and that was it; and it sounded rough. With that in mind, after a flying visit to Peterborough, we took the van to a well-known Ford dealership in Birmingham to get it fixed. We were told it was the crankshaft; it would have to be changed. And we would have to pay. What happened to the warranty, I don't know. I can't remember how much the bill was, but we picked the van up and promised to return the next day with the money. Unfortunately for the garage, we left for Germany the next day, so the bill was never paid. Serves them right for selling us a duff van to start with. But all the same, we had to steer clear of that dealership for a while.

This trip to Germany was much better. Baumholder is not too far from Frankfurt and a lot closer to Zeebrugge, and we had a van that went well. That is apart from when you tried to put it in reverse too quickly and the gearstick would pop out of the cogs, which meant having to unscrew the gearstick and lining up the cogs with a long screwdriver. Not good when you had a stream of traffic behind you.

The venue this time was the sergeant's club on an American army base. It was an R & R camp, so there was never much military work going on, as most of the men were there for a rest after serving in Vietnam.

The camp was on the outskirts of the town of Baumholder and we stayed in a small hotel in the town. The hotel was very small, and we had the top floor (three rooms). It was such a small hotel that it didn't even have hot water—the reason I grew a beard, as shaving in cold water is painful.

One of Griff's postcards home from Baumholder

On our first day at work on the camp, we had to report to the camp commander, a colonel I think. He didn't like us. He didn't want any 'long-haired hippies' on his camp. He told us, if we wanted to work there, we would have to have our hair cut. No chance! We refused and were then told that we would only be allowed on stage and in our dressing room, not in the club; and we wouldn't be allowed to mix with the men. Not a problem when you consider that, as we drove onto the base, every single person we saw had hair that was at most a quarter inch long, and that included the women. So we did stand out a little.

He then asked us where our girl singer was. What girl singer? Another wonderful management move. We were supposed to have a girl singer, which was a surprise to us. We didn't even know any girl singers. We offered to dress Alan up, but no.

Anyway, we were eventually supplied with a girl singer; I don't know from where, but she turned up. Her name was Jean Lyons. She was Jamaican and very

petite. She had quite a good voice but no stage presence at all (not that we did). We would play a few songs and then introduce our female singer, Jean, and on she'd walk with her handbag, put it down by the mike stand and sing her songs whilst not moving anything apart from her mouth. The only songs I remember her singing were 'To Sir with Love' and 'Do You Know the Way to San Jose?' We later found out that she was pregnant—by none of us I hasten to add. Maybe that's why she didn't move a lot.

It wasn't long before we were allowed out into the club and to mix with the GIs, which was quite scary at first. They were all bigger than us, and of course, the hair thing didn't help. I think some of them were jealous because they couldn't have their hair long. It's strange really because, by today's standards, our hair wasn't really that long. Mind you, it did get longer as the weeks went by, as none of us ever had a haircut.

The GIs were, in the main, a good lot, with just a few odd ones who were stuffy. We overheard one guy telling his mates that, if he didn't get a girl soon, he was gonna have to have one of the group! Luckily, we were friendly with most of the guys, so it didn't worry us. It was quite an eye-opener working in the club. It was like being in America, using dollars and watching American TV. We saw Star Trek a couple of years before anyone else in the UK and learned how to play shuffleboard with the GIs.

We also learned about 'happy hour', when drinks were half price. And didn't we take advantage. It must have been quite a sight seeing all those drinks being lined up on stage, and I mean a lot of drinks, and that was on top of the drinks the GIs would buy us. No wonder we don't remember much.

It was an NCO's club, so you had quite a mix—from hillbillies to junior officers who came in suits and ties (though not many did that). On the whole, it was quite casual and even more casual when we went into the club.

The club was a revelation. It was the first time we had seen 'proper' coffee on tap 24/7, and you could get a meal at any time. The cook was a tall thin guy who was always smoking and used his top pocket as an ashtray. It was strange working on the base and living in the town, as, in the town, the currency was Deutschmarks and, on the base, dollars. We also had some English money, so it was very confusing.

The place was full of interesting characters. There was an older guy who always used to request 'Together Again' and wore snakeskin boots. When we asked him about his boots, he told us they were rattlesnake and always used to say, 'Rattlesnake eats a man.' God knows what he was talking about.

We got friendly with quite a few of the guys in the four weeks we were there. A couple spring to mind. Owen Smett was one. He was a regular solider, not a conscript, as a lot of the others were. He was supposed to do a two-year posting in Vietnam, but after a couple of weeks into his first stint, he was badly wounded and had spent eight months in a hospital in Japan. He was wounded by 'friendly fire'. Why they call it that I'll never know; doesn't seem very friendly to me.

He told us he had been slightly wounded whilst on a night mission when his platoon had been involved in a firefight with the Vietcong. The medics thought it best to get him back to the base hospital to be treated in case his wounds got infected. Whilst waiting in a clearing for the helicopters to arrive, they came under fire from the opposite side of the clearing and called for helicopter gunships to help out. Unfortunately, when the helicopters did arrive, they shot up the wrong side of the clearing, killing or wounding most of the GIs who were there. Owen was lucky; he was only wounded.

When he recovered, he went back to Vietnam and, after a couple of months, was wounded again and spent another few months in Japan. That was how he spent his two-year posting. He showed us his battle scars—not nice! There wasn't much of his body that wasn't scarred.

Another guy who comes to mind was a Mexican, Johnny Robbles. He was quite a small guy and a tank commander. He used to come to the hotel most mornings to get us up (late nights, lots of booze, you understand). We never minded him coming, because it was another pair of hands to push the van, which always refused to start in the mornings.

During the breaks—we used to get about thirty minutes after an hour on stage—we would go across the base to the EM (enlisted men's) club. There was a big difference in the clubs. The EM Club was mainly coloured guys, who were into soul and funk, and they would dance around having a good time. The sergeant's club was mainly white guys, who were more into pop and country and western and looked smart and didn't dance that much.

The EM club had a band called The Twigs. Half of them were German, and they had a girl singer (of course). I think they had been there for some time and knew the stuff the guys liked, so they were very popular. When we went in the club, they always seemed to be playing the same couple of songs, probably because we tended to go in at the same time most nights. Anyway, the songs were 'Tighten Up' and 'Memphis Soul Stew'—great songs, and they played them very well. They would then normally have a break, and we would get to chat to them. It was in one of those chats that I made a big mistake. I swapped my Fender Precision for their bass player's Epiphone Rivolli. It seemed a good idea at the time. But it was heavy and woody and sounded bad; still, it looked a million dollars!

They told us about a beer festival that was on in a nearby town on our next day off. It sounded like a perfect day out, so on the day, we set off for the beer festival. On the way there, we stopped at a yak store, which is like a wooden hut on the side of the road that sold booze. We bought vodka and whiskey and carried on to the festival.

The festival was in a very large marquee with long wooden tables and benches and an oompah band blasting away. We were told in no uncertain terms that liquor wasn't allowed, so we weren't allowed to take our booze in. Fortunately, Dave Toy managed to push it under the edge of the marquee, so we got it in anyway. What with the beer and spirits, we all got very drunk, which seemed to be normal for us then.

Dave Toy was driving and decided to drive on the left, stating, 'I'm English. We drive on the left.'

It was very scary, but luckily, the road was quiet. I think he only made two or three cars go off the road, but he was too drunk to care.

Ray had gone missing, and we found him on the floor of the van, so we used him as a footrest. I have an idea someone threw up on him as well. I know we had to carry him upstairs and put him to bed.

We were told by our management that our next gig, straight after Baumholder was in a town called Trier, which is on the German/Belgium border. So on our next day off, we went there to check out the club we were booked into for a four-week stint. The band that was playing there was a German band. I can't remember their name, but they weren't very good. I just remember them singing a Lee Dorsey song, 'Working in a Coal Mine', as 'Vurkin un Der Coal Mine'. It sounded very funny sung in a strong German accent. We were told a couple of days later that the gig had been cancelled. They probably didn't like the look of us. So we were booked to play in Hamburg instead.

One of the best things about the sergeant's club was that big name acts came over from the United States to entertain the troops. While we were there, they had the Shirelles and the Toys. One of the girls in the Toys fell in love with Griff's *coat—unfortunately not Griff, just his coat. It was a regency styled highwayman's coat, and he ended up swapping it for her fur coat and $5. Good deal?*

While we were in Baumholder, it was Dave Toy's twenty-first birthday, so we went into town to celebrate at a hotel where a lot of the GIs went. We knew quite a few of them but not all. We all got quite drunk (unusual!) but Dave was probably the worst out of all of us; well, it was his twenty-first.

The problem was that he kept going into the cloakroom and coming out with a different coat each time; most of them belonged to the GIs. Well, Dave was small, and most of the GIs were big. So he was generally swamped. That wouldn't have been so bad if he hadn't paraded around the room saying, 'Who am I?' and just dropping the coats on the floor and then going back to get another one. Some of the guys were getting a little upset at having their coats thrown on the floor. But because we knew a few of them, we managed to escape with our lives.

There was a nightclub in the town that was off limits to the GIs. But they still went in there, and it was very popular with the coloured GIs. We were in there one night with a couple of them when the place was raided by the MPs. They didn't just throw the GIs out and arrest them; they really laid into them with batons and beat them up quite badly. We just legged it with the GIs we were with, but it was awful; there was blood everywhere. We found out later that the MPs were quite racist and that, if the GIs had been white, they would have just been arrested.

It was at Baumholder that we got our first taste of what was to become quite a common occurrence—American guys coming up to you and telling you they had a famous relative. For example, they were Otis Redding's cousin or James Brown's brother or some such thing. Normally it would be, 'Let me up on stage to sing, and I'll put you in touch with whoever it was,' or, 'I'm a producer/manager/agent. Sign with me, and I'll make you a famous,' or some other such thing. Well, the first *couple of times you get taken in. But after that it was more like, 'Yeah of course you are. Now f*** off.' But later that year that would be our downfall—our 'almost'.*

We must have gone down OK at the base because there was talk about us going to Saigon for a couple of months to entertain the troops there. Then, however, there were some Vietcong attacks in Saigon, so it all went out of the window. Shame really; that was our luck. There was also a gig in Beirut in the pipeline, but they decided to have a war.

We used to play up to the fact that, when we went abroad, things seemed to happen. The first time in Flensburg, the Czechoslovakia takeover happened. When we were in Hamburg, there was trouble in Poland. And around the time we were in Paris, the student riots were going on. We'd tell people we weren't really in a band; we were SAS but couldn't talk about it. No one believed it, but it was a bit of fun. Or was it true? You'll never know because we can't talk about it!

Anyway, our time in Baumholder was at an end, so we set off for Hamburg and the Top Ten Club on the Reeperbahn.

Chapter 5

Hamburg

We arrived in Hamburg direct from our four weeks in Baumholder in about September 1968, which meant missing my sister Polly's wedding. Fame—who would have it?!

The Top Ten Club was on the Reeperbahn, the main road in the area of Hamburg called St Pauli. A lot of the big names from the early sixties had played the Top Ten, including the Beatles. It was just around the corner from the better-known Star Club, which no longer exists but, at the time, was still buzzing. The Top Ten Club is still there, but it's not called the Top Ten anymore.

We were contracted for four weeks and were living in the Park Hotel, Lincoln Strasse, just across the main road and up a side street from the club. It was a very busy road, and no one liked crossing it. It was dangerous, and I don't think drivers liked to stop for you because it was a very rough area. We heard that there had been three murders within five hundred yards of our hotel within a few weeks. So drivers were nervous about stopping to let people cross the road. We used it as punishment if someone did something wrong—make them cross the road to get some fags or whatever.

Talking about fags, we used to put shilling pieces in the fag machine instead of one-mark coins; it worked out a lot cheaper. The fag machine people must have sussed that it was all the English groups playing at the Top Ten putting the shillings in the machine.

The club was quite small, with a bar down one side, tables and chairs scattered around, and a small dance floor. I think our dressing room was downstairs, as were the toilets. In the entrance to the toilets, in a kind of reception room, sat an old woman behind a table selling condoms, toilet paper, sweets, and drugs. The woman was known as Mutti (Mother), and she was well known to lots of people. She would tell us stories about how she looked after the Beatles and the like, and she was mentioned in various books about the Beatles. If you went downstairs looking knackered after coming off stage, she would give you a couple of pills to keep you going—Captagon—an amphetamine! You ended up having to buy more and more to get the same effect—clever old bastard!

The stage was small for seven of us, and the floor of the stage was coloured glass that lit up as we played. We had to use the club's PA system, and it was controlled by the management, as were the amps and so on. No playing too loud!

It was very hard work. There were always two bands, and you worked one hour on, one hour off, starting at 7 p.m. and finishing at about 6 a.m. weekdays and 7 p.m. to 7 a.m. weekends. The bands took it in turns to start first. We often used to go to a disco just up the road when we finished playing to unwind with the barmaids and waiters from the club; the waiters also acted as bouncers—not to be messed with! St Pauli was an area where there were bouncers and doormen at every club who would grab you and throw you in, I know that sounds strange but true, they throw you in to the clubs to make you spend money!

We used to get to bed at about 11 a.m., sleep until 5 p.m., get something to eat, and go back to work. Some days, we used to go to the club in the afternoons to rehearse. The manager, a Scotsman named Ricky, was a sax player and would sometimes get on stage with us to play. 'Peter Gunn' was his song, and the crowd used to love it.

Talking of the crowd, the first Friday we were there, a lot of girls came in to the club from out of town and all stood at the back of the club, deep in conversation. On our break, we got friendly with them and found out they were deciding who in the band they were going to 'have' and for how long! It worked out that, every Friday and Saturday, they would come in, and we would be theirs. One I remember was called Gudrum from Kiel.

In the week, we were free agents. I remember early on in our first month there, Ray and I chatted up two girls who were dressed in suits like men. Their explanation was that they played in a girl band at one of the clubs, and they all dressed as men to turn on the punters. That sounded feasible—until we got back to their place and found pictures of naked women all over the place. They promptly went to bed together and left Ray and me to watch. Very nice, but not what we had in mind.

The weekends were the roughest. In St Pauli, there was a curfew. No one under eighteen, I think it was, was allowed in the area after 10 p.m. Every now and then, three or four policemen would come into the club and walk around with their batons drawn. And if there was anyone who looked young or they didn't like the look of, they would poke them with their batons and ask for ID. This caused many fights.

On one occasion, they poked a Scottish sailor who didn't like being poked with a baton, and there was mayhem. Our usual reaction was to just leg it and let the bouncers sort it out.

Some days during the week, when we didn't go clubbing, we would help Mick repair his sax. It was unbelievable how many rubber bands he put on it, which he used instead of proper springs for the valves. He would walk up to the end of the

Reeperbahn to a repair shop that was above a house. We once tried to learn the song 'Memphis Soul Stew', quite a medium-paced song, and asked Mick to play the solo. He asked if he could use the solo he played in 'Seven Days Is Too Long', a really fast song. That was Mick. He used to get girls to dress as men so that he could get them into the hotel. I don't think it worked very often, as the hotel was quite strict about taking girls in.

After a couple of weeks, our manager in London called us and told us we were going to Munich straight after Hamburg for a six-week gig. We didn't really want to go, and Griff and Alan were pining for their girlfriends, Libby and Anita. Griff was the only one who used to phone home regularly. That was a big deal in those days and was quite expensive—love, hey.

Anyway, we told our manager no. He got quite nasty and said we had to go. Well, that wasn't the thing to say to us, so we just refused. He then said he would come over with some of his heavies and make us go. He came over, but because we were well in with Ricky, the Top Ten manager and the bouncers, it didn't work. Instead, he left us with threats of death and told us we would never work again. Scary, really! When we arrived in Dover on the way home, we were quite nervous that he would be waiting with his heavies.

We had been to the Top Ten Club previously when we had a couple of days in Hamburg after the Flensburg saga, so we knew the club and had met with Ricky, the manager. So when we went to the club on our return to Hamburg, we had some idea of what to expect. What we didn't expect was to see our old boss/singer from way back when, Jimmy Powell. He was there for a month and had been there for two weeks already so had another two weeks there with us. He was the same as ever, a likeable rogue. Unfortunately, we still never got the money that he owed us out of him. But I do remember us all sitting in his hotel room smoking and wondering why everything seemed so hilariously funny.

There were a lot of drugs around at that time. We were offered a fifty-kilogram block of marijuana for a £1,000, which was an awful lot of money, not that we had any money anyway; but then, it was an awful lot of drugs.

Jimmy was in the same hotel as us, the Park Hotel. I think he had a room to himself, him being the big star that he was—or used to be, as he had a top ten hit with 'Sugar Baby' in about 1961. His band, a five-piece, must have shared a room. They were from Newcastle, and we had met them before in Jimmy Powell's Northfield Studio, so we would meet up with them and go round to the Ning Po for banana fritters.

I must explain about the Ning Po. It was a Chinese place in one of the back streets behind the Reeperbahn. It was an odd place, but it was cheap, and the food was good. I used to have liver and onions, not very Chinese but very filling, or a curry for the equivalent of about five shillings. I suppose we would go there once or twice a week.

The other place we used to eat at was right next door to the club. I can't remember the name of the place, but it was more like a coffee bar come café type of a place, and we would go there quite a lot after work (it was open 24/7, as were most places on the Reeperbahn). We always had the same thing, goulash soup with a chunk of bread. This became our staple diet; it was great!

The other good source of food was the German equivalent of a burger wagon, selling bratwursts with a bread roll, sauerkraut, and mustard—heaven.

At the Park Hotel, we shared two rooms—Dave Toy, Mick, Ray and myself in one and Griff, Phil, and Alan, the other. Two things I remember are Ray spending about an hour before going to bed picking his spots and blackheads and Alan running up and down the corridors with his pyjama bottoms pulled up over his shoulders bent forwards. He looked like an escapee from a lunatic asylum.

The hotel wouldn't allow us to bring girls in, understandably, so they had a *doorman who used to keep an eye open for us trying to sneak them in. Mick's efforts to get girls dressed as men in worked once, and he spent the next couple of days telling us how wonderful he was in bed. Mick was older and more experienced than the rest of us, and he thought it was great that he had kept his 'rocks' on; rocks was Mick's word for socks. He loved getting people with his 'chokers' (too hard to explain). But the last time we saw him thirty-five years later, he was still trying to get us with his chokers.*

Mick is the only one of us that hasn't kept in touch. Unfortunately, Alan drowned while on holiday in the early '80s, and Dave Toy died in 2017—a great shame. Two great blokes and bandmates.

A couple of things happened in Hamburg that could have changed our lives forever in very different ways. The first was Ray once again falling in love, this time with a prostitute from the Eros Centre, an indoor marketplace for prostitutes and anything else sexual you wanted—and I mean anything! But remember that prostitutes were legal in Germany and had regular health checks, so it wasn't as bad as it sounds. And most were very good-looking, with figures to match. The prostitutes in Hamburg were provided with their own bouncers for awkward customers.

When Ray decided it wasn't love after all and told her it was over, she didn't like that and came round to the club one afternoon when we were there. That wouldn't have been so bad, but she brought two of her bouncers with her. She was mad as hell. She ranted that nobody dumped her and so on. Most of it was in German, but we got the gist of it. And most of it was directed at Ray, but she blamed us all. It was then she threatened us with death at the hands of the 'boys'. And they would have done it. Make no mistake; they would have done it.

In the end, Ray managed, with our help, to talk her round. And off she stormed, taking her two boys with her. Now it sounds funny, but at the time, it was scary.

The other potentially life-changing thing was meeting a man named Ed Chalpin. We had never heard of him. According to him, though, he was head of Polydor Records in Germany, a German company but very well known worldwide, with quite a few big names with recording contracts, including the Searchers and early Beatles. He wanted us to record a song in Germany and then go on to the United States of America and record an album. He told us he was Jimmy Hendrix's manager and could make us stars. Well, he must have been about the tenth person in a couple of months who was well connected or had famous relatives who were going to make us stars. We thought about it for ten seconds and basically told him no to the German record and said that we would think about the USA bit, and that was that. We went back to the normal (if Hamburg can ever be described as normal) daily routine.

That, folks, was our 'almost'. Chalpin phoned us from the United States later that year when we were at home and asked us to go over there. Well, we had no money for travelling to the USA and asked him to send the money over for the fare. He told us he would give us the money when we got there. Well, this to us was another one of those, yes-of-course-you-will moments that we had had a number of times before, so we said no.

It was about six months later that Alan turned up to a gig with a copy of Melody Maker. Inside was a picture of a top producer and manager with one of his acts, The Animals or Jimmy Hendrix; I can't remember which. You guessed it. It was Ed Chalpin, who we had met in Hamburg and had basically told to f*** off. Almost.

One evening in between sets, I was in a car just off the Reeperbahn near the Star Club with, I think, Ray and Dave, and a friend of ours, a girl who worked as a prostitute in the Eros Centre, when a police car pulled up near us. We were very nervous because we didn't have our passports with us, which meant we could be arrested, not recommended with the police in St Pauli. After about two minutes, two policemen got out of the car and walked across the road in our direction. They took out their truncheons and laid into a woman who was walking down the street, minding her own business. They gave her a real beating and then dragged her into their car. Unbelievable! We later found out that this 'woman' was really a man who was wanted by the police.

There was a street in St Pauli called Herbert Strasse. It was unusual, in so much as it had a steel door at each end of the street with bouncers to stop underage boys going in and to throw drunks out. The street itself was about fifteen feet wide, with houses on each side. Each house had a bay window or picture windows, and in each window was a woman, all in various states of undress. It was probably the biggest brothel in Europe.

As I mentioned earlier, because of the long hours we worked, we were taking quite a few uppers (amphetamines) and downers. One kept you awake, and the other put you to sleep. The end of our stint in Hamburg arrived, and our last night at the club was great. We had been very popular at the Top Ten Club, and the punters were great on the last night. We had a five hundred-mile drive the following day to Zeebrugge and our ferry home, so we behaved ourselves—except Ray, who had his uppers, as we all did to keep going. But Ray, in his wisdom, decided to take sleeping pills as well when we finished the set. The problem was, when amphetamines wear off you become very tired; and with the sleeping pills as well, we thought he was dead. We couldn't wake him up. But as he was breathing, we decided to set off anyway.

We had a passenger on the trip, a girl who we had gotten to know who wanted a lift to England to visit friends. She was very thoughtful and brought sandwiches and hard-boiled eggs. Ray, although still alive, was dead to the world—so much so that his head provided a convenient place to crack open the hard-boiled eggs. The only time he woke was when he wanted to go to the toilet. And then we had to take an arm each to help him and had to hold him upright at the urinal. I can assure you we only held his arms; we were close but not that close!

I can't begin to describe the smell in that van. Seven men, five with hangovers, and a woman with hard-boiled eggs cooped up in a Transit van for twelve hours—unbelievable.

When we got to customs at Dover, we were, as normal, pulled over to be searched. But when the customs officer knelt in the van, his knee went into a packet of rancid butter that Ray's mother had given him on our first trip to Germany three months earlier. With that plus the smell, he very quickly extracted himself from the van and told us to f*** off, which was lucky for me because I had a packet of amphetamines in my pocket. Knowing that Dave and I would have to drive the van the five hundred miles to the port (we never took roadies abroad), I thought they would keep us awake. I had put them in a fag packet, which I threw away thinking it was just an empty fag packet. I never sussed it until about fifty miles further on. What a waste.

We were expecting our manager and his heavies to be waiting for us as, as he had promised, but thank God, he wasn't.

So ends the Hamburg chapter, and the French adventure begins. Onwards and upwards.

Chapter 6

Paris

I hope this little journal doesn't give the impression that we only worked abroad, as most of our work was in the United Kingdom. Some would say that the UK work was our bread and butter, and our overseas work, the jam. Not too sure about the jam bit, but the work in the United Kingdom was our living—in Scotland, Wales, and all over England for not much money but lots of fun. It was all for one thing—to 'make it'.

Our next trip over the water was a little closer to home and a little shorter, about two weeks. It was Paris, gay Paree—good food, nice people, the good life, and so on. Well, it was great if you had loads of money and spoke French, but we didn't and couldn't.

The Parisians were not very friendly and quite stuck up as we found out, and Paris is very, very expensive. Having said that, it was quite a feather in our cap, as the main gig was at a very famous café in Paris called Maxim's. It was Maxim's anniversary and was coupled with a film premiere after-party, with quite a few celebrities there, including Richard Burton, Elizabeth Taylor, Prince Rainier, and Princess Grace of Monaco. How we got the gig I can't remember, as we had fallen out with our management in London because of our refusal to go to Munich.

Anyway, we made the papers. The press release said, 'The group Whiskey Mac are flying out today to play for Elizabeth Taylor etc. for the anniversary of Maxims in Paris which is also the venue for the after film premier party.'

The truth was we were all piling into the van for the 'flight' to Paris. We went via Dover to Calais and again, as usual, were stopped by customs at Calais but, unusually, were let through within minutes. We went into a café just outside the docks and decided to have a bowl of soup each; as normal, we were all broke.

I remember Ray saying, 'Leave the ordering to me because I took French at school.' He then proceeded to order the soup in English but with a French accent— funny. We left the café and headed down the road to Paris; we were to meet our agent's French counterpart in Paris, who would then look after us and act as our guide and translator. Unlike our previous trips abroad, where we had worked in one place, in Paris, we would be working all over the city.

We were about twenty to thirty miles down the road when we were pulled over by the police. Speeding? No chance. Along with the police was a carload of customs men. We were ordered out of the van, and the boys in blue then proceeded to take all of the equipment out of the van and take it apart, all on the side of the road. Luckily, there was a small grass verge, and it wasn't raining. After about half an hour of searching the van and its contents, they uttered some kind of what appeared to be a threat or whatever that we didn't understand (even Ray who spoke French!) and drove off leaving us to put everything back together and reload the van. Needless to say, we were late meeting with whatever his name was. I'll call him Pierre.

Pierre's favourite saying was, 'If you can't get a woman tonight youmust be gay," but we thought the Parisian women were very stuck up.

After our meeting, Pierre took us to our hotel, a very small family-run place just off the Champs Elise, close to the Arc de Triomphe. I think the man and his wife who owned the hotel weren't that pleased to have us there and stuck us in rooms on the top floor out of the way. I remember my room overlooked a sewage/ waterworks—nice view, if you're into sewage works, not too smelly. The hotel, as I said, was small and seemed quite narrow and high. The reception was about ten feet from the front door, and the stairs (there was no lift) were right in front of you. They were very narrow stairs that kept turning back on themselves, a bit like a spiral staircase but not as nice; it was so narrow you couldn't walk up the stairs side by side.

Our first gig was in a nightclub in the centre of Paris. The club was downstairs under the street, a weird place, all flashing lights and the like, very dark and dingy—a typical nightclub really. It suited us, as there was a disco that played our kind of music, James Brown and lots of soul music.

We were told it was being filmed for some TV programme, so there were lots of men with cameras and microphones. I remember a man walking around with a bank of lights strapped to his back following the cameraman around. We played our set and made silly faces to the camera every time we were being filmed—very sixties, but lots of fun. The set went down well, and everyone seemed very pleased with how it went. Unfortunately, because it was for French TV, we never did get to see it. It was shown on TV the day after we left.

The next night was the 'big gig' at Maxim's, where all the rich and famous went. Well, they certainly did that night—Liz Taylor, Richard Burton, Princess Grace, Prince Rainier, lots of them. But we missed most of it because we were backstage.

Maxims

Les 60 ans de la PUCE à L'OREILLE
Les 75 ans de MAXIM'S
Vendredi 18 Octobre 1968

✳

CARTE DE SERVICE

✳

M   *Terry GILL*

~~vous êtes prié de vous présenter à   heures~~
~~au Cabaret des Ambassadeurs 3, avenue Gabriel~~

My Maxim's pass

It was a bit of a farce really. There were lots of different acts on. The act before us was a swing Sinatra type band, very good but totally different to us. We were told there couldn't be a break in the music, so we had to get on stage with the swing band and gradually take over. Well, you can imagine the scene—a swing band in full flow dressed in tuxedos, and Griff walking on in a red frilly shirt and so forth, sliding on the seat vacated two seconds earlier by their drummer and trying to play swing with the rest of the band. Multiply this by seven, and result—chaos.

It turned out OK in the end. At least we got paid and were fed. I think the most disappointing thing was that we never really got to see the famous faces, let alone meet them. The best we got was a quick glimpse as they went out. You couldn't really see much from the stage because of the lights, so I couldn't even say that they ever got to see us.

Driving in Paris is bad enough at the best of times. The Parisians didn't seem to care very much about their cars; most were scratched, dented, and generally wrecks, so they didn't care if they collided with you. Having a Parisian as a guide made it worse. And having the steering wheel on the wrong side made it worse still. We had to rely on the passenger in the front seat—in this case, Pierre! His idea of good driving was that you'd indicated it was your right of way, even if anything was coming, so none of us wanted to drive. We would toss a coin, and whoever lost had to drive. It was scary, and how we never had a crash is amazing.

Because we were only working at night, it gave us the days off. Remember, we didn't get up until late morning, and during the day we were tourists seeing the sights. One day, we decided we wanted to see the Bastille, so we ventured into the metro (subway), you could buy a ticket and stay down there all day, which we normally did because we were always getting lost. We finally got to the Bastille by the roundabout route, only to discover they had knocked it down years earlier and built an office block or something similar. The only reason you knew you were there was a little plaque that told you so.

On another day, we went up the Eiffel Tower. In those days, you could look through the telescope at the top, and a guy would come round and collect money for using it. It so happened that we were faster than him at running around the top of the tower, so we never did pay.

We were told by Pierre that we were playing one night at a private party at a very flashy hotel in the city centre and that we had to be there early to set up. When we arrived, we were given a dressing room behind the stage and were told that, after we'd set up, we were to stop in the dressing room and not to venture out. Pierre would see to our needs, food, and the like.

Well, he certainly did that. We had fantastic food, the best Paris could offer, too good for the likes of us. In fact, it was duck à l'orange we found out later. But at the time we didn't know what it was and didn't fancy it, so it ended up all over the dressing room after being used as ammunition in a big food fight. We just stuck to the champagne that Pierre kept bringing in. God knows how much we drank, and I don't know how we got on stage. But somehow, we managed it.

It was quite late, and we could hear music and things going on. It sounded like an orchestra playing at the front, and indeed it was. We went on stage behind curtains and waited for the cue. The orchestra stopped playing, and some bloke rambled on in French, apparently saying there was a surprise present for the host of this lavish party.

We got the nod and started playing. The curtains opened, and there was this very large, very flashy and crowded ballroom. And we were the surprise present.

There were quite a few young people, student types, in the crowd, and Alan or someone must have said something to them because they all got up on stage with us.

It was difficult to move it was so crowded on stage, but with all that champagne inside us, we really didn't care.

I believe we did another gig very similar a couple of days later. Again we were the surprise present, and again, as normal, there was lots of good food and champagne; I could get used to this. Then it was back to the hotel and a sword fight up the stairs with sticks of French bread stolen from the party, much to the disgust of the landlady who came out and shouted at us in French. We couldn't understand a word she was saying, but she was obviously very annoyed and threatened to throw us out.

One day, we had to travel to Abbeville, a town about forty or fifty miles outside Paris. So we had to get up early, with a little help from Pierre, and drive to Abbeville. I can't remember much about the gig or the trip, but obviously not much happened, or I would have remembered.

We were only in Paris for two or three weeks, but it seemed longer. We had a good time there, and it seemed easy after the German gigs. We only had to play for a couple of hours, and we had food thrown in, sometimes literally. Pity we couldn't have spent more time there.

After arriving back home, we were offered a residency at the Club Cedar in Birmingham. The dressing rooms were upstairs and were reportedly haunted. We never saw any ghost or anything like that, but it was quite eerie up there. As well as playing with a few well-known bands at the club, we got very friendly with the barmaids, who always gave us double measures when the bosses were not around.

I think that, by this time, we realised we couldn't carry on having no money, and we had no real prospects of 'making it', so Griff and Phil decided to leave and get jobs. The rest of the band carried on for a few months with a replacement drummer, Kex, a nice guy and good drummer. He later joined Magnum and found fame and fortune. Sadly, I learnt that, in 2010, he developed a brain tumour. A lot of the local bands organised a big gig in Cannon Hill Park to raise money for the Cancer Trust.

But this wasn't to be for us. We eventually finished and all joined different bands with different levels of success but no fame or fortune. From 1964 until 1970, we had a lot of good times—some bad, but mainly good. And I can honestly say that I wouldn't change a thing. Well, maybe the fame and fortune bit and the fact that I'm now quite deaf and have raging tinnitus. But we made good friends, friends for life. And as for the fame and fortune—well, almost.

Chapter 7

The Reunion

In 1998, we decided on a reunion visit to Hamburg, which was great fun and brought back lots of happy memories from thirty years earlier. Unfortunately, our friend and singer Alan Devy drowned whilst on holiday in Spain in 1981, and we couldn't find Mick. So the troop consisted of me, Griff, Dave, Phil, Ray, Sam, John Parkes, and Charlie, an old friend of the band. We even managed to stay in the same hotel, the Park Hotel.

John and Dave outside the hotel.

The Star Club was down this street on the left.

The Reeperbahn. The Top 10 Club is on the left.
The Top Ten Club was unfortunately closed. But when we explained
to, I think it was, a cleaner who was in the club at the time that we
had played there in the '60s, he very kindly allowed us in.

Dave, me, Griff, Phil, and Ray sitting on the Top Ten stage.

Leaving the Top Ten Club.

Star Club

The Star Club no longer exists, but the original building
is still there with a plaque to commemorate it.

A break for one of our many liquid lunches. Phil made the mistake
of ringing the bell, not realising that, if you rang the bell, you bought
a round of drinks for everyone in the bar. A bit of a shock!

Charlie, Ray, Sam, John and Dave.

Well-Known Bands We Worked With

Them (Van Morrison)	The Alhambra Club, West Bromwich
The Fortunes	The Plaza, Handsworth
Heinz and the Wild Boys	The Plaza, Old Hill
Slade (twice)	The Ship and Rainbow,
	Wolverhampton
The Drifters (a few times)	Club Cedar, Carlton Club, Plaza,
	Handsworth
Chris Farlowe	Durham University
Geno Washington and the Ram Jam	Durham University
Band	
Gary Farr and the T Bones with	
Keith Emerson	Durham University
The Scaffold	Nottingham University
The Move	Club Cedar, Birmingham
Trapeze	Club Cedar, Birmingham
Idle Race	Rainbow Club, Birmingham
Robert Plant and His Band of Joy	Frank Freemans Club,
	Kidderminster/
(Led Zeppelin)	Birmingham University
Family	Carlton Club, Erdington
Earth (Black Sabbath)	Smethwick Baths
Chairman of the Board	Walsall Town Hall
John Mayles Blues Breakers	RAF Abingdon, Oxford
Nashville Teens	Wolverhampton Civic Hall

Dave Berry	Plaza Handsworth
Swinging Blue Jeans	Molyneaux, Wolverhampton
Crispian St Peters	Plaza, Handsworth
Duane Eddy	Plaza, Handsworth
Plastic Penny	Club Cedar, Birmingham
(two members went on to Elton John's band)	
Marvellettes	Walsall Town Hall
Johnny Johnson and the Bandwagon	Walsall Town Hall
The Toys	Baumholder, Germany
Shirelles	Baumholder, Germany
Moody Blues	Plaza, Old Hill
The Hollies	Birmingham Ice Rink

Below are a few pages from our 1968 diary as you can see very

busy and the vast amounts of money we earned!

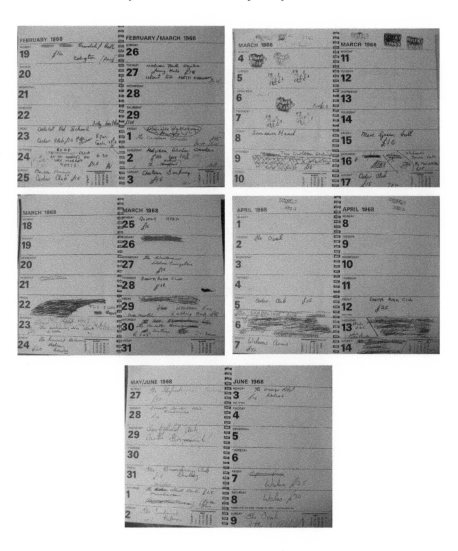

Well, that's it.

The end.

*All that's left is for me to thank everyone
who helped put this journal together.*